BURNING OF THE THREE FIRES

Burning of the Three Fires

POEMS BY

Jeanne Marie Beaumont

JEANNE MARIE BEAUMONT

*For Mane,
for our love of poetry &
book culture — your book
next? Right? At the Front
Place once again —
with pleasure
Jeanne*

AMERICAN POETS CONTINUUM SERIES, NO. 124

BOA EDITIONS, LTD. 〰 ROCHESTER, NY 〰 2010

First Edition
10 11 12 13   7 6 5 4 3 2 1

For.information about permission to reuse any material from this book please contact The Permissions
Company at www.permissionscompany.com or e-mail permdude@eclipse.net.

Publications by BOA Editions, Ltd.—a not-for-profit corporation under section 501 (c) (3) of the United
States Internal Revenue Code—are made possible with funds from a variety of sources, including public
funds from the New York State Council on the Arts, a state agency; the Literature Program of the National
Endowment for the Arts; the County of Monroe, NY; the Lannan Foundation for support of the Lan-
nan Translations Selection Series; the Sonia Raiziss Giop Charitable Foundation; the Mary S. Mulligan
Charitable Trust; the Rochester Area Community Foundation; the Arts & Cultural Council for Greater
Rochester; the Steeple-Jack Fund; the Ames-Amzalak Memorial Trust in memory of Henry Ames, Semon
Amzalak and Dan Amzalak; and contributions from many individuals nationwide. See Colophon on page
96 for special individual acknowledgments.

Cover Design: Daphne Morrissey
Cover Art: "Skirt Triptych" by Jess Robson
Interior Design and Composition: Richard Foerster
Manufacturing: Thomson-Shore
BOA Logo: Mirko

Library of Congress Cataloging-in-Publication Data

Beaumont, Jeanne Marie.
 Burning of the three fires : poems / by Jeanne Marie Beaumont. — 1st ed.
   p. cm.
 ISBN 978-1-934414-40-8 (alk. paper)
 I. Title.
PS3552.E2318B87 2010
811'.54—dc22

                              2010009193

NATIONAL
ENDOWMENT
FOR THE ARTS
A great nation
deserves great art.

BOA Editions, Ltd.
250 North Goodman Street, Suite 306
Rochester, NY 14607
www.boaeditions.org
A. Poulin, Jr., Founder (1938–1996)

State of the Arts

NYSCA

CONTENTS

Trinket

Alteration of Girl

Rites

With gratitude to my forebears,
& especially to John "Jack" Beaumont (1916–1999)

Trinket

An awe came on the Trinket!
—Emily Dickinson

What is your favorite flower, favorite bird?
I really want you to tell me. If you had twins
what would you name them? Or two goldfish?
How about two cats from the same litter?
Mittens or gloves?
What letter did you most love learning to write
so when you scripted it over and over in your copybook
you tingled with graphic pleasure?
Pick a crayon. What's the best time of day?
When you play Monopoly,
which little token represents you on the board?
Have a seat. This could take a while.
Cup or mug? Placemats or tablecloth?
Would you rather live in a world where no one cared?
When you were six, what was your favorite song?
It's sad to forget. Uh huh.
What suit of cards do you prefer? Which fairy tale?
Seashore or mountains? You must choose your horse
on the merry-go-round or you can't ride—a lesson
of long ago. What were the most comfortable shoes
you ever owned? (Here I could tell a strange story;
let's just say I have evidence—somewhere
there's someone who could fill your shoes exactly.)
What do you want for dinner?—speak or starve.
My head hurts too.
As it happens, you've stumbled
into my humble democracy.
Here's your cup of coffee, your violet-blue crayon,
your miniature iron, your hummingbird . . . ,
now, friend (if I may call you friend),
let's get to work.

TOTEM

I remove my watch only to bathe. Because I'm fastidious,
I'm a good baker, a good proofreader. "Eagle-eyed,"
mother would say. I like measurements. Measured time
passes more slowly I tell a watch-shunning friend. If you
swung by my place at 3 A.M., you would see my light on.
Don't phone me before noon. In 1970 I stayed up all night and
tripped into another world. Part of me came back ruffled.
On a Tuscan garden patio, I heard a cuckoo call and thought
it was a clock. If I could afford it, I'd buy that *casa*. I am a
time bomb. Not one of those early birds that gets the worm. Who
wants the worm? It has us soon enough. One May day in Cornwall
I watched a robin hop o'er the grass cocking its head. Heard the
worm, it did. Next had it beaked like a bit of linguine. Gone
in no time. I saw a hawk snatch a squirrel right out the crotch of a tree.
In Central Park, where the swing chains cry like gulls. I am that
squirrel, that grey without Clairol. My mother's totem is owl.
My niece's, giraffe. The word totem comes to us from the Ojibwa.
My sister dislikes depictions of cows, which are ubiquitous in
Missouri where she lives. She's named Charlotte after our grandmother.
My brother's Jay. My cousin says paintings of rabbits bring luck
to a household. I have 133 cats in my bathroom, two live ones.
Cats sleep 18 hours a day. Last week I bought a painting of ghost-faced
little owls on a wire, above them a branch with a bird, or maybe two.
Is that a cardinal or a red leaf? My father was a cardinal man.
The painting is titled "4 Good Omens." I wish. But time tells
the only stories we can live. Just between us, I am afraid to fly.

THE BIRDBATH, OR
NOT MY USUAL ENTRANCE AND EXIT

Mistakenly, as a bird that flies
    in the window. You remember that
        fiasco, the resultant broken tea-

Pot, scones crushed into the Persian,
    sprained ankle that nagged you
        for months. Admit one.

Admit one reason you fail to arrive
    is a lingering negative association
        with this avian air.

From the crosspoint of the garden paths
    the bath regards the sky from its post,
        it keeps an eye on wings.

I hear whispers about my
    "attractive nuisance." What might it
        breed? White flower frozen in full-out

Bloom, liquid-centered like Belgian chocolate
    or a properly baked soufflé.
        Part baptismal font, part

Giant's goblet. Shallow as summer,
    as neighbors. I've christened a few
        of its regulars for the games we play

(God bless 'em!). Even a vicarious sip's
    enough to rinse the pervasive
        bitterness from my mouth.

I forgive, evenly, you for the missed
   frolics, the dispersing flocks. This
      morning tolled as the first of many

Or the first ever morning
   when the world hatched new.
      Squirrels ribboned a parcel of lawn, one

Butterfly opened its coloring book
   on my cast-iron chair.
      Raucous twittering as Jack of Spades and

Pick-up Stix splashed in their bath.
   Chirpy. As a virtue. You don't think, do you,
      I could be too old to learn?

FLOWER & CAMERA

(Flower & Camera Day, June 29)

Suppose
an f-stop for flowers
a bud's shuttering open
a bulb's flashy
eruption
each posy as pose
move in close
say say freesia or
chincherinchee

style is part of a flower
naturally
a rose is a pose
even in repose
likenesses multiply
all colors smile
when asked
bring on those
floriferous machines!

Oranges

i.

One day out walking in the park I saw an orange at the base of a tree. Like a child's ball abandoned when the child's fancy drifted elsewhere. A reject? An offering? Was someone so sated the orange had to be left behind? Was someone so burdened the orange could not be borne any further? Had it slipped from a bag and rolled to a stop there, an orange on an accidental adventure? Large egg laid in the grass by a colorful bird, sheltered by the tree. How hungry would a person have to be to pick it up?

ii.

Along the same path, I spotted another orange, but this one turned out to be just the peel, carefully restored to its original shape. Any trash bins in sight? No. Maybe a clever imbiber had tried to disguise the garbage. Maybe the chick had hatched. A bright and perfect sphere except for one excised section, giving it the provocation of a cubist sculpture. Its orifice spoke of use and appetite. Its skin was situated so that sunlight poured into its interior through the torn aperture. Two oranges, like two tenses. Would there be a third?

iii.

Not in the park, although I kept my eyes peeled. It was later, crossing the street on my way to the subway, that I noticed the skin of an entire orange flattened on the macadam like a map of an orange planet. Steam-rolled, it extended eight inches at least. It made me happy to think that a fine orange coat could be tailored out of it by some tiny orange-hide-using tribesman, who might also fashion pants, or the soles of his shoes. But he had better retrieve it soon—there was a lot of traffic.

Going by Taxi

I wear gloves to my elbows; you wear herringbone trousers.
It starts to snow; the streetlights haven't switched on yet.
I lack ordinary patience; where's the towne crier?
   You say correction; I say retraction.
The citrus look exacting; they make calm orange pyramids.
Let me buy alstroemeria; you choose the beer.
Wood bundles whiten near the awning; remember our fireplace?
Life takes things away from you; the snow gives way to sleet.
   You say umbrella; I say imbroglio.
Tuesday's best for sleuthing; we pursue the stubborn missing.
When I'm needy, I'm rude; keep an eye down the avenue.
We don't want to let that taxi go by; we don't.
All this time yields no evidence; all this time gives no clue.
   I say angry; you say ennui.
Let's kiss when the meter starts; ah, here come the lights.
I've forgotten the address; you've a claim check in your pocket.
We stocked our coat closet with wood; it was ten, eleven years ago.
Bugs crept out under the door; carried far from earthy homes.
   You say step on it; I say no stop.

We don't know the tune on the radio, and the street's turned black
       with snow.

Fancy That Does Not Do But Is

(Dagobert Peche 1887-1923, Neue Galerie)

The box is a bird. Jeweled, impractical.
        The elongated Lady Chair
                not for a lady, *is* a lady
as the desk is a castle.

How many flowers are too many flowers?
        A scarf field. A wall field.
                Solve no problem.
The bird is a box.

In such elaborately framed mirrors
        you would never be the fairest
                would be, in fact, never more
than plain

but here nothing is dulled
        by the chilly touch of facts,
                why a kind curator has hung them
too high to peer into.

As for the exquisite bird box
        we bow to behold it.
                Beside it a silver pumpkin
with gilt interior

viewable only to its occupant.
        A container detains what it retains.
                Attention. A little keeper.
For pleasure

as we walked in the snow
        to get here. Crossed the park.
            Crossed the century
weary of utility

to dream of a self
        detained in an extravagance
            that has no earthly use
for us.

Dressing Table, 1963

bobby pins of remorse   the comb of discretion and ardor   hand mirror
of inquisition   curlers of docility and demure tendencies   tweezers of a
wished for perspicacity   perfume flirtation   the lone caterpillar of mascara
lipsticks of indecision or wax fruit   safety pins of excess   the blush of
tenderness, its brush with density   small scissors of mordancy   a powder-
puff of inflammatory rhetoric   deodorant of encoded reason   nail file
of rectitude and civility   a tissue of gallant intrusion on its bed of
anaesthetized kin   the pin cushion of perpetual devotions   the barrette
of carnivorous tenacity, its snap to attention   jewelry box of extinct
populations and jaded humor   smelling salts of admonishment   cream
of vanishing certainties   one red rouge eye   tiara possibility in the
drawer   twin frosted   lamps of diplomacy
it keeps appointments   wears a pleated skirt

A Vienna Postcard

Ah, the bliss of standing alone in the *puppen* museum
examining a wall display of small and smaller shoes!
When a loud couple came in—that thoughtless man
puffing a cigarette—I squeezed into this dollhouse
and hid in the attic. Their stay was brief. Why had they
bothered? The more minute an object, the longer
it takes to study it. I purchased this picture so I
wouldn't forget my escapade. (On the right's the eave
that sheltered me.) Outside, the glare of a giant sun
set my eyes to rapid blinking. I needed a bathroom—
such dilemmas of the flesh! It pains me to record that
in the end, despite my hours of admiring attention,
not one of those dolls would lend me a comb.

In Pursuit of the Original Trinket

trin·ket (trĭng′ kĭt) *n.* [Origin unknown.]

From the crossroads (L. *trivium*) of my travels
I transported these home
From the third-world market of trivial not-junk

Plink, plink, plink onto the tabletop (imitative?)
Does any thing fit?
Appearing as from a magician's trick cabinet—

    a triad of pink piglets
    a trivet too <u>dinky</u> to be of use
    triplet kittens linked by a minuscule chain

    a three-car train to ring the rink of the rail set
    third-rate stones that blink from an anklet
    (clink of junk jewelry, e.g., *a trinity of bracelets?*)

And here's a thin pen with three tones of ink—try it.
A tri-part ticket to amusements (triple your fun!)
Or, in which a trio sings a minor minuet (*Meet the Trinkets?*)

Less than you think, an inferior trink, possibly.
It's barely a trickle. You can't really drink it.
A tin ring kit. A trinal locket—or even clarinet.

Which brings us to that instrument
one plays by heavy petting: I won't be
your strumpet number three (i.e., "la trinkette")

When you trifle with me—wink wink wink—
I can't wing it, kid, I'm trying to forget.
Perhaps mere ornament doth make us tristful?

It's still trite even if you ink it. Did someone shrink it?
Yet, no word is an empty valise.
How could it not be

of three things I (returned from said junket)
take out of the trunk,
the tiniest, saddest, and most girlish, hence *trinket*

A Notion

From one perspective a coat had lost its button; from another, a button had lost its coat. Lots of buttons, lots of coats.

In the beginning, six buttons had been attached securely to a small card, and the card had hung in the Notions Department. In the universe of buttons, *securely* is a relative, precarious word.

The button had at one point been sewn securely to the coat. A seemingly excessive number of passes of thread through the holes, a sturdy knot, etc. Yet at once the at-first-imperceptible loosening—the loosening that leads to loss—commenced. But often a person with a loose button treats it cavalierly and won't do anything about it. Lets it hang by that thread for days, like a book read up to the next-to-last page. The button has to free itself entirely and at a moment when it will be most conspicuous, clattering onto a hard floor or bouncing off the back of a small dog—yip!—if it wants to be saved. Luckily for those legions who depend upon them, most buttons do.

When she noticed the button dangling from his coat, she had a notion to yank it off and end its torture. It was unfortunate, unfair, that the rather hardy button had to be dependent upon the weak, constantly fraying thread. A classic marriage of unequals. The coat itself was just a neutral background against which this drama of thread & button was played. The tight-lipped buttonhole arguably shared some of the blame. And what about the fingers of the man, who so often and without thought or care had manipulated the button through the hole? Often in great haste (she could imagine him) as he reached home eager to shed the day, the weather, all that's outside, his fingers would pop each button like one striking quick notes on a bass fiddle. Did he start from the top or bottom? Who would be waiting for him to make his fingers move so rapidly that now as she pictured it, a viscous blurring, she felt she might faint?

It was at that moment she reached to grab onto the button—just as the subway doors opened and the man turned to exit. As her head cleared, she found she clasped the button securely in her hand. But, as mentioned . . .

An Instantaneous Production

Two adjacent corners connect by a grey thread, making a square. An accordion joins a small band, starting toward it from the opposite end of the street just as the band arrives in the square. A loop is made. It is possible next to pull the thread, draw the corners tight together, and fold the band into a two-inch packet. Enclose in a kind vest pocket. The thread must stay attached. You will hear a faint drumming all day like a second heartbeat—isn't that wonderful?

Later, at the edge of town, you can tug the thread, release the band, carry it between your hands and set it down, where it will seem to appear *instantaneously*. To much certain applause (with a little practice). The most important item is the thread. Choose carefully the thread. It must be strong enough to bear the strains.

DOLL WINGING (THE CICADA DIED A NATURAL DEATH)

The wings are veined with glitter glue

  The wings are made of fine magenta tulle

   The wings are formed with fake flower petals

     The wings are crafted from turquoise painted rattan

      The wings are shaped with wire and glued to sheer fabric

        The wings are removable

        The wings are cotton and nylon embellished with sequins

       The wings are made of organza burnt with an incense stick

      The wings are adorned with passementerie and bijouterie

     The wings are sewn with hundreds of seedbeads

   The wings are fashioned with found feathers

The wings are made from real cicada wings

Broken Dolls Day

(June 3, Japan)

The stitched would never
heal. Nor could the smallest finger

missing of a hand be glued to a pudgy
plastic palm. She lies on her back—*bye-bye*

It is over. Around her those of the lost
screws, stuck eyes, detached

wires, burnt hair, punctured torso;
brother work, dog work, left out

in the rain. Played out. Over the wood,
wax, plastic, porcelain, papier mâché,

straw, leather, resin & cloth,
the four-foot hunchbacked monk

bows his ancient bald head.
O broken ones, we are

the careless world—forgive us
for we wore you as ourselves.

ALTERATION OF GIRL

Reading a Road Map

You must start
with a longing

                  choose a compass point

along the blue route
that leads

                   back to childhood

ignore the cargo
left by the highway

                  plunge ahead

with your
forefinger trace an artery

                  to the nearest juncture

you think you couldn't
be happy there

                  but here's compassion—

roadways web
in every direction

                  threadlike the rivers &

railways criss
& cross

                  no one is missing or lost

I shall read
your silence

                  as a space on the map.

⌣ Cocoon

I don't know when or where
I was conceived. In our house
we didn't speak of such things.
Before that, another infant girl
had joined the family, briefly,
staying under two weeks.
If I'd been able to, would I have said:
deliver me there, to that family, for I see
they are sad, that the teenaged daughter
is sweet yet unhappy, the boy clever
and sadly quiet, that the mother is very sad,
and I can help although for years
her sadness will glom on to me
making our passage difficult and strange.
In our house we didn't speak
of things such as the miscarriages
that also occurred before I arrived
but weren't disclosed till decades later.
Make no mistake. How much we wanted
each other, no one can say for sure.
Photos will verify that father had
a glimmer in his eye, that he loved
nothing more than to bounce a baby
on his knees or raise one in the air
until a shriek of pure glee was released.
If not, I offer my word. Here's what
I do know but cannot remember:
the summer I was born was terrible
with mosquitoes. In a borrowed crib
I lay, I slept, I woke within
a white gauze of netting. I'd been
the heaviest at birth of mother's four,
and I was being protected. Watched.
Though no one believed it yet.

I wasn't going away. We were all in it:
mother, father, sister, brother.
When I fussed, the netting parted
and one of these would take me up.

GAL LORE

Gal (găl) *n. Informal.* A girl. [Alteration of girl.]

i.

Galactic
        she makes the stars come out
galactic, a milky way

a buxom blond cowgirl on afternoon tv:
      it's *your gal Sal*

      (tip of a five-gallon hat)

she's showing Popeye, she's showing 3 Stooges

sipping, the young girl, the milk of the sponsor
nipping Nestle's Quik,
            milk through a straw

little cowgirl vest, fringed skirt
                  pointy boots
and holster, yes sir. *Bang bang pow.*

      A real lil cow gal pal
           —how now Sal?—
watching Sally Starr
             astragal: a type of molding

ii.

Grail: mutation of gal and girl
Gallant one.
Galahad most purely
Had a gal too
Surely?

iii.

as one sculpted
by being spurred
     girl on Sunday gal on Friday
        gala by Saturday night

and so by this she gallops year to year

quick quick   as though electric
from a galley,
     through a gallery
        to a galaxy (very near)

connecting the dots
     is it a girl?
    is it a grail?

It's a gal
     galoping   (the late discovery of guys)
       gallivanting

        galvanizing

   gal: a unit of acceleration

used especially
for values
of gravity.

Valiant gal
    glad when she lands
to be the answer to her own prayers

A Childhood, B.C.

Mary had a little doll that she'd found in a cave when her brothers took her on one of their expeditions. It was carved of hard wax with matted lamb's wool for hair, and she loved it more than the caged birds in the garden, more than the smell of bread, and sometimes more than her rowdy siblings. But when her father caught her cradling it, his fury coiled and struck—*We keep no graven images in this house!* He grabbed the girl's idol and heaved it toward a nearby stream. Mary kept her eye on the beloved, who floated face-down bobbing slightly. When no one was watching, she waded in and made her rescue with the aid of a broom. She swaddled the doll in linen and carried it under her blue shawl until she came to a cedar tree with a hollow she could just reach now that she was eight. After tenderly drying the body and tangled hair, she tucked her bundle up in the tree. Each day she visited, warming the doll against her stomach and offering olives and dates. She placed a necklace she'd threaded of mustard seeds over its head. She whispered where its ear should be. A secret. Someone was watching.

From the Annals of Perseverance

Bent over overlapping *O*'s of the copybook

                Between Cleanliness and Self-control (—traits)

. . . in spite of failure

                        "picked yourself up brushed yourself

Oaf shook the table, spilling/

                spoiling the meniscus; she rose

    to fetch the pitcher and filled the glass again.

  Unquiet nights in steerage

  unquiet stagecoach

              Proceeded down a long aisle:

    managing the crutches managing

to crack the code not breaking the code not then

                        Rewards of the method drone.

Slogging through   (much later?)

                    . . . in spite of fright *really*

    submitting over & over & over

  Drip, it drips, has dripped, will keep dripping,

          Tying knots with frozen fingers

  >Bitter End<

          Penning the linked O's better!

For which the child earned an A*

SCREENED-IN PORCH

You'd have to choose a summer night
when everyone's home. When father didn't have to go
back to the car dealership after dinner
and a Phillies game was carried on the radio.

The Bakelite box radio's been moved from the kitchen
to the porch step. Except what's cast
by a 60-watt living room lamp, the porch is dark.
You can't tell that plastic weaving on the aluminum
furniture is red and white, but you hear how

the glider chair creaks, creaks as the daughter,
desultory, pushes off with the rubber tip of her sneaker.
The outdoor carpet, a dense super-thick felt,
softens the concrete slab only a bit.

Brother hasn't enlisted yet. Nightly they sit,
listen to the cicadas' long ascendant waves and fade-outs.
The leaves of the maples and wild cherry
shuffle in sporadic breeze beyond the screen.

Tonight, you'll listen to the Tastykake jingle or
Black Label whistle break the inning's top from
bottom, as mother, done with dishes, sinks
into the remaining chair. *What's the score?*
She mock-groans when she hears and longs for

a menthol cigarette. Her husband sips a can of beer.
Brother clears his throat, or it's his snort, a form
of not unfriendly commentary he perfected in his teens.
The shortstop fumbles, picks up—too late—
the ball to get the runner out at third.

Judas Priest, father mumbles, who knows
the corrosive effect of small errors. The glider soothes
the young girl. The air smells deep green.
Her mind waits far in right field, dulled by that

wait. Haven't you come to tell her
she's having a happy childhood? A bat cracks.
A thwarted bug thuds against the screen.
It's so quiet, no one hears you leave.

Xho remembered her lessons in the use of scissors.
Xho cut smoothly and evenly so the edges were not jagged.
Xho brightened her needle with an emery bag.
Xho made matching pockets to keep potholders.
Xho won the bodkin race, pulling her ribbon most quickly.
Xho doubled her hems as she had been instructed.
Xho was not one of the four in ten children who died by age six.
Xho sat on a low stool while sewing.
Xho put her needles back in their hand-shaped needle case.
Xho saved her fabric scraps for her mother's quilting.
Xho would retreat into domestic life to flourish unseen.
Xho is known to us now as Helen P., *the first in her class to finish her apron.*

RECOLLECTIONS: AVIARY

Your first name
but not your last

My pert ponytail
like a girlish puppeteer's
one of my good (sane) years

springing to life in the middle
of the episode
moving the mouth by the hand

The scarcity of furniture
Not your look

but the large empty aviary
in the center of the apartment

Song it held once
not its silence

Not how I acted
but what it took.

New Wives' Tales: Index of First Lines

A girl kept a small bird who could sing in Japanese.

All day the woman had stood by the hydrant staring at their house.

A rack of hangers, she thought, a rack of bones.

Forty-five years and nary a bump in the night.

In her experience, the weather rarely cooperated.

It wasn't that he snored, but when.

Lies were the foul chicken coop of her years.

My sister left home because she didn't want to breathe here.

She couldn't whistle anymore, or rather, she wouldn't.

She'd as soon throw the skillet than scramble his eggs in it.

She never forgot the day her mother pulled out the black apron.

Sunday was the woolliest day of the week for all of them.

The battery life of her watch was a constant worry.

The child clutched her hand, who had no friends.

The rug was unraveling after she'd worked so hard on it.

The thoughts in her head and the words from her mouth had parted company long ago.

Under the sycamore, she began to count and sweat.

Who cooked in heaven, she often wondered.

Why was he home so early and where was his car?

Poor Shoddy

shod·dy (shŏd′ē) *adj.* [Origin unknown.]

She's odd.

She's nobody and knows it.
She shudders, all shook up
      in her shabby body
      her shunned body.
Can't shed odors of a shady past,
a shaggy dog story of shitty odds,
      a soggy shack, slipshod
      shanty 'mid the sodden sod.
A sure lock on schlocky. Come up short.
What's sloppy is near ungodly,
      what's odious should be shot.
      Should die. Should she? Shhh . . .
Such damaged goods
the source of Schadenfreude.
      Shocking. Her show of shards.
      What a lot to shoulder.
Shut the shutters, shadow lady,
shut the shouting out
      (ah, but not the shame)
      the stab of an age-old jeer
that seems to call your name—
Cheap shoes! Cheap shoes!

_____LESS

Twas then I came to stand under the solemn fact
that missing some part made one monstrous.
Eye-patched, peg-legged—cried failure to keep a self intact.
Maimed added misery to fate's cruelty. Thus I stuffed
lambswool into kid gloves to fashion—I liked to say

perfect puppet hands for lacing to my wrists.
Escorted to the opera, one of the rapt dark audience,
I passably clapped my part, then hid the kids
in my black mink muff and smiled, as mother advised,

to *keep all eyes on your face.* To think this whole time
you were galloping toward me, sir, over meanwhile's miles,
a terror to towns though elegantly dressed. When your

cape swooped, enwrapping me, I knew heart's fullness
could trump mindlessness, knew to hold tight with my legs

let myself be seen entire with your brainy hands.

BRIDE

I was long dead before you singed me.
I sat bolt upright, got back my yodeling form
    and shocked the castle cats. Before my lightning 'do
struck you down hard to cobbled floor,
    a boxer overmatched, I was vacant socket.

All men are monsters, mother crooned.
    The night before I was buried
I dreamed a surgeon
    tweaking my body like a transistor radio.
I never felt a thing. Many things at once.

    And these are my blood lines, which creeked
out of the core of the Carpathians,
    lapped to a dry rust stain by the large
predatory birds that dwell in crags.

Some kind one conducted my heart
    back to its basal rhythm.
Oh screw me tighter or I'll come
    undone.

MA BELLE

A thinking woman sleeps with monsters.
—Adrienne Rich

A rose began it
               you got it, father
but you don't
               get it
A rose begat it
               my own fur-bellied fruit

               Appearance is only
a door to peer through
               to pass through
                              Once admitted
one paces the corridors
               hearth-warmed

He trundled toward me
               proffered his chaliced heart

A rose has many doors
                    a   maze   spreading
and beauty
          turns our heads
                         and duty pulls our legs
and we are all
          torn

The rose began it
                    tailbone tender with latency
     near-whiteless eyes
                    equipped for night
suckling one such
                    grandkid, father

Adore   these pelaged eartips
                                        see into this pea-
shoot heart to find
                            our family resemblance:
It bends without breaking
                                    It climbs the walls

Is Rain My Bearskin?

Pssst.
          I'm the blonde in the shower
water too hot   water too cold
          ahhh
                    No one gave me
                    the key
I picked the locks and made myself
          at home in the pantry

My belly's distended   worn
          one moment on fire   one moment on ice
I emptied the honey pot
                    cooked up all the spam
spit it out
          had to eat a box
of nice cookies to kill the taste
          of the chowder I chowed down
                    once I'd found
a proper porringer   the right-sized spoon
a chair that
would bear
my heft
without crashing
          (it only grumbled a bit)

I'm the freeloader   thief who stole day from night
          one too dark   one too light
Look
          I've used up the sham-
poo scouring my fur   for the final act
                    I crack
                              the safe
run off into the pelting rain
          counting the gold that clangs in the satchel

                           wrong   wrong
Grrrrr   who am I in the story
                                    I'm just right
This time the car is waiting
                    I get away with everything

Your Sign Is Digger

I packed my bag and stood ready to leave in two directions—
Having just come down from the coast of my excess.
You used a shady answering service that spoke in relative terms,
"I'm your mother," for example (Freud disliked the phone).
She'll get back to me.

In a dream I smoked the peace-pipe with my father.
I must have slept on the worry side of the pillow.
Come to your senses:
Does periwinkle blue mean anything to you?
This restaurant makes exceptional breaks no breads.
It's breakfast.
Circumstance for which I'm always last to arrive.

On the subway platform a man held a book in one hand,
A hook where his other hand should be.
I tried not to look.
This wasn't a dream so means—nothing?
Salsa music cascaded down the nearby stairs.
(If you've got time, I'd like to kill some dancing.)

How else does exertion become exhaustion?
The letters, letters, letters.
It's not true that objects can't embarrass you.
Unpack my bag, or the tomb of my mind where I buried—
Don't wake the dead, they're unprotected.

But your sign is Digger. What is it you seek?

This must be where we redeem our jarred-up pennies for thoughts.
A pen for your thoughts (Freud had no typewriter).
In red ink on a periwinkle sheet:
"Dear _____, About that dream . . ."
Too bad I never could read your homewriting.

WHAT SHE CARRY

(after John Currin's "The Lobster")

Her burden   the table worn   her back   her
burden   the drapery   upon it   her burden
the loaf of bread   jug   or pitcher   of wine
no picnic   this mother load   this massive mass
precarious mound   of nipply lemons   *lemonade*
dear? first aid dear   for a body   bent o'er to
near breaking   her burden   the preposterous
hat   her bother   the in-your-dreams-catch fish
heavy-eyed   looking to slip   off & out   careful
sister carry   for us all   don't spill   tilt   let fall
stay *still!*   her burden   big Lobster   blood-red
centerpiece   of the scene   its carapace   mean claw
her burden   the violin   its bridge   varnish &
scroll   she must be   in shape   to bear   *who*
framed her? such instruments   long centuries of it
that she   lean   that she carry   be   and hold
that she   display   say   dish   jugs   folds   skins
bounty   curves   all without losing   her hat
feast her burden   the crusted loaf   the fish
in shell   the fish in scale   the yellow fruits
the thing with strings   the weight of glass
the bunched material   the weight   oh hell
the pain   the pain   the paint   the paint

GIRL ON A SCALE

Winter drew in.
I watched food fall away
from her mouth

no, it was a dream
my daughter stood on one foot
like a seabird by my bed.

I sat up insisting
but birds eat constantly.
Outside the frost

a sapling, stalk, a reed encased.
What use, to refuse?
Not a gain again.

Ungrown so thin she slipped
between the bars
and hunkered

inside her cage.
Then the fur came upon her.
Then the one

with icicle teeth
who eavesdropped on our silence
masticating air.

I awoke—it was she in the bed,
toward her
the IV dripped dripped
like an early thaw.

Taper, or
Mary Tells All She Knows

A string to me says *spine*. I am patient
in long labors. In taking pains.
Dip, drip. Let them hang.
Repeat the steps.

I adore the odor of beeswax each day.
Authentic & pure as I suppose a
martyr would be. I'm none.
At dusk,

I light the tallest all along the stone mantle.
It is true I am a wisp of a woman,
smoke comes out my mouth,
my head heats up,

and sometimes if I hear a word that's especially apt
my eyes bounce like breezed flames.
But you shouldn't confuse
me with them.

These were born in the clean shrine of tedium
to accumulate evenly, cane straight.
Burning, they fly the flags
of thin victors.

And when they disappear—as is written—
leaving behind them no trace,
this is no miracle but ex-
pertise.

I think about the past. I empty the ice-cube trays
crack crack cracking like bones, and I think
of decades of ice cubes and of John Cheever,
of Anne Sexton making cocktails, of decades
of cocktail parties, and it feels suddenly far
too lonely at my counter. Although I have on hooks
nearby the embroidered apron of my friend's
grandmother and one my mother made for me
for Christmas 30 years ago with gingham I had
coveted through my childhood. In my kitchen
I wield my great aunt's sturdy black-handled
soup ladle and spatula, and when I pull out
the drawer, like one in a morgue, I visit
the silverware of my husband's grandparents.
We never met, but I place this in my mouth
every day and keep it polished out of duty.
In the cabinets I find my godmother's
teapot, my mother's Cambridge glass goblets,
my mother-in-law's Franciscan plates, and here
is the cutting board my first husband parqueted
and two potholders I wove in grade school.
Oh the past is too much with me in the kitchen,
where I open the vintage metal recipe box,
robin's egg blue in its interior, to uncover
the card for Waffles, writ in my father's hand
reaching out from the grave to guide me
from the beginning, "sift and mix dry ingredients"
with his note that this makes "3 waffles in our
large pan" and around that *our* an unbearable
round stain—of egg yolk or melted butter?—
that once defined a world.

Burning of the Three Fires

(June 30, France)

i

I set the cookbook on fire
by holding it close to the
reading lamp

ii

I began the reading lamp fire
by holding it close
to romance

iii

I lit the romance by
holding it
close to the cookbook

RITES

until it snows winter is dull and cruel until the sun rises certain birds won't sing until
the cat eats she is ultra-attentive and vocal until it begins to rain I am content to walk
until the next day we exude garlic until the butter is churned nothing else can happen
until twine is plucked from the streets weaving is a dangerous endeavor until a plumage
of diplomacies the bleating of iambs echoes until the border screams at me I don't
appreciate its displacements until the check comes we enjoy our meal until an alarm
goes off symptoms of discontent go unnoted until a remedy is found reconciliation is
devoutly desired until the spring arrives in our parts it is too cold to send the heart
back to its rightful owner

Four Seasons

(after Brice Marden)

spring

daffodil yellow the ground and

over all the spread the sprawl

of green spent until every corner

was green & I sat yellow-young

a green thought a greed let's

you and I spend lazy on the

green blanket and dandelions

breathed beneath us we could

barely count minutes we had

not yet learned to count years

summer

darker than we imagined was

an ocean swelled a deep blue-

green deeper than any forest

it held us   and washed   us up

a hammer and an arrowhead

and smooth bottle tiles every-

thing currently altered by it

bored smashed rusted ground

and the sea always   near then

the lone salt   giving change

autumn

I must be there fog in the vale

grey time as we pulled out of

town rain grey like the roots

or the mug of an old black cat

salt & pepper here dear

headed where the fleet

fleetingness of the years blear

beloved dull wool jacket

lull in the wood sky shelf dust

in a pantry salt in the drawer

winter

you have had three of four to

the end you have read it is

late black starless night no-

thing getting through no step

closer deepest indigo go in

dark velvet threshold large

fabricated door believe you

might be able to pass through

but not yet you stop keep

for now space be tween you

REMOVED: A MEDITATION

. . . all things that are, are equally removed from being nothing; and whatsoever hath any being, is by that very being, a glasse in which we see God.

—John Donne

A glass is an appliance
used in many ways, for instance
a medicine cabinet mirror
on which an insect
pauses
providing simultaneous views
of its front and back.
I'm the fortunate looker.
See four wings set like a pert bow
on the quarter-inch package
of its body. A present,
it cheers me enormously.
Because downtown
is burning and burning

and how to go on but
a step, a segment, arc of a circle—
"There are but a few Circles,"
Donne writes, "that go about
the whole world." I believe
at least a weak black thread
must attach each one.
Thread like the edge
of this tutu of wings,
these pliéd legs.
And God must be
a consummate miniaturist.
Of course. But,
God in a tutu?

Yet this is how our plots unfold.
I & Insect
—who visits nightly and lifts
for a few speculating minutes
my melancholy—
equally removed from nothingness,
regarding each other in the glass.
For Donne's melancholy
pigeons were applied to his feet
to draw vapors down
from his head. Imagine.
Donne's first glimpse of God
in the pigeon-glass.
It would please the bird.

Rite (to combat a bad mood)

1. Remove the word *rabbit* from the word *hat*.

2. Turn the pig back into the porcelain.

3. Wake the mother tongue asleep on the roof.

4. Tell my ills to go. Madame, tell my ills . . .

5. Fill the vacancy on the swing.

6. Be there when the bread comes out of the oven.

7. Scraps happen to have their uses.

8. The floor is a problem that must be carefully solved.

THE HOOKED GIMMICK

This made of dying,
This small sharp hook at the end.
At one end.

This body tube of coming and going.
To be a tube that rolls—
The right hand over the left arm, or
Picked up altogether very often
To be thrown with a silken movement (caught).
Loaded with many such movements.

This make of dying with some
Gimmick—stoppage blockage lag lump seizure choke stroke
    gag snuff lack sting shot collapse crack crush—*presto!*
The gimmick is the taking skill.
It may be concealed in the tube beforehand.
The hook of it deep in the inside.
Bent in the body.
Caught in the cloth.
Or held in front.

      Thrusting its head, the body advances.
      Its silks spin and dance.
      Then the hook appears
      Talks the silks out of the tube entirely.
      And the wand of air is passed through it,
      Proving it empty.

As If Nothing Happened

for Joe Bolton 1961-1990

Twilight now and on a crooked deck, a boy-
man handles his scotch, the burn of its amber
entrapping what bugs him, what squirms then stops
squirming in the scrutinizing heat.

The ribbed glass presses wetly to his palm,
sweat of languor, of in-between, and he smokes
as a siren slices the traffic down
its middle, shoulders bulging to make way.

It's not hard to imagine a body
rocked on a stretcher, hearing fading out,
because he's long practiced, to imagine
the self all gone, or everything else   —that

swift passage through the yielded corridor—
then cars merged back in lines and driven away.

Mixed Tulips

Infant-skinned, crayon-hued tulips,
carried home with Sunday's heavy news-
paper, bobbing jostled buds
in bright silk dresses, in communion-white tulle,
you hardly make a fuss
held up in a green glass vase.
One glows red as a clown's nose and one's
small and pink as a doll's teacup, but
you are by origin Ottoman,
tulips, you are the folded turbans
enwrapping the mind of the tulip god.

As you open I find the curved chambers
in which I would like to be carried from this world.
Drawn-petal-curtained rooms,
gathered in the grass-green vase,
a mansion of blooms faced out
toward the doorway, unfurling your flavors
more and more to the bright day.
You taste of earth's secrets—
what beetle has rested in you?
What upright souls do you offer
like hatpins from a great aunt's purse?

Soon, soon you will bend
and perform your Salome act,
unloosing your rainbow of veils.
The ruffled yellow slips will fall
and the regal purple sleeves will
peel off one by one by one.
Oh tulips, you make grand company.
Who will throw you out at the end,
pick up your petals like severed tongues
from the shelf, dab the golden pollen
that was your final excretion?

Who having outlived a few bright flowers,
who able to let go of connections to the past?
For surely we tire though we must not,
having breathed the godly air of tulips
to the last.
Is it only to be dreamed—to be borne
from this world inside a sanctuary of tulip,
red, pink, yellow, purple, white or whiter white?

Rite (for quitting the premises)

For one who owns the bewilderment
of departure

no circumstances are ordinary.
Scarve the neck, protect the ears.

On the way to displacing your
self-bundle of electricity

tender letters, tip the porter.
Underappreciated, your essential character

accompanies you. Through each turn-
stile, a quelling, a refuge awaits.

In tumult of transit
something inadvertently's bound

to be lost or left.
First near, then far.

Symptoms of disconnect
may be treated with longing—

beyond reconciliation
for its own sake.

The sweet distress of longing
never was truant.

Earnest announcements are
entering you. Allow them to.

You must be more careful. You must wash your hands up to your elbows and dry them with a linen towel. You must say please. You must swallow your lumpy medicine. You must draw a card and return it to the deck. You must deny deny deny. You must put it in writing. You must write your name on a cup and pee in it. You must read *Moby Dick*. You must read *Moby Dick* again. You must perform forty hours of public penance. You must eat your spinach and finish your milk. You must shave. You must do windows. You must name names. You must demonstrate your ability to parallel park. You must share. You must lock the door and leave the key under the mat. You must change diapers. You must sift the dry ingredients and fold them into the wet ingredients. You must learn to work around the pain. You must drop a sack of unmarked bills in the trash bin by the sweetgum tree. You must forget what you just saw. You must produce your passport when asked: *now*. You must slip into something more uncomfortable. You must revise. You must, for your own protection, put on the blindfold. You must reset your clock. You must let the dog lie at the foot of the bed. You must pay the piper and leave a generous tip; use exact change. You must burn the dark letters. You must bail some water. You must forgive your mother. You must march to the river's edge. You must stop crying. You must give away your possessions to the poor. You must soak in bleach. You must pledge allegiance. You must summon the energy to clear the last hurdle. You must be very very brave. You must click your heels three times. Wish to be removed from this list, moved from this list, emptied of all words.

[EXIT CORPSE]

When you are the only extra
from some manic-depressive hamlet in the black heart of Prussia
standing in the middle of a huge silence
like the date on a tombstone
a piece of dust
      you can't go any further

Their first time everybody's scared to death.

When I made my wan entrance
      like the negative of a person
      a soul in the hall
      a standing joke
      obliged to wear a lurid costume in each new scene
I said, in the same sepulchral tone
speaking straight out of my own bones
Blue makes me laugh.
After that I felt safer.

What I couldn't stand was this shrinking
      head of a hatmaker's dummy
      white mask for me to wear
      ghost pale in the dark air
      shaking those seedpod rattles . . .
("Acoustics," he said.)

In a room with four cadavers
      the zombie rose up in my throat
If I slept, it was with my eyes wide open,
if it turned out to be somebody awful—
I shivered.

The dust cleared, and I had a full view of the battle.
I had fallen and could fall no farther.
                              "Poisoned."
The grey scraps were ferried off,
        the chill gripped my ankles.
                "I'm going I'm going I'm going"

                [The soprano screak of carriage wheels]

Channeling Sylvia: 8-Ball (Interrogation)

Is there ennui in the afterlife?
  YOU MAY RELY ON IT

Can you still see the moon?
  REPLY HAZY TRY AGAIN

Can you still watch the moon?
  AS I SEE IT YES

Do you regret the oven?
  IT IS DECIDEDLY SO

Do you still compose poetry?
  IT IS DECIDEDLY SO

Is *Ariel* now as you would have wanted it?
  CANNOT PREDICT *NOW*

Sorry, is the restored *Ariel* what you wanted?
  MOST LIKELY

I get the feeling you've not really been able to see it, am I right?
  REPLY HAZY TRY AGAIN

New topic. Have you seen your father?
  YES DEFINITELY

Was he upset by "Daddy"?
  YES DEFINITELY

But he's forgiven you by now?
  YES

Have you seen Ted?
> YOU MAY RELY ON IT

Sylvia Plath, is this really you answering?
> BETTER NOT TELL YOU NOW

Should I keep writing?
> MOST LIKELY

Was it all worth it, for the poems?
> IT IS DECIDEDLY SO

Are any of your lost journals still in existence here?
> WITHOUT A DOUBT

Are they in a trunk?
> REPLY HAZY TRY AGAIN

Were they saved in a trunk?
> YOU MAY RELY ON IT

Will I live long enough to see them revealed?
> DON'T COUNT ON IT

Thank you. I think I've bothered you enough.
> YOU MAY RELY ON IT

(11/2/06, All Souls)

HAIL

Sylvia! the fruit you are
offering to the fruit of your womb
is poisonous

though it looks like a globe
of far golden continents,
a delicacy pinched

between your slender
finger and thumb.
You wear the blood-red cloak

and halo of spiny needles.
You've let down your rank hair.
Yet the child propped

on a pillow extends
too small a hand
to grasp the deadly orb.

I pray from the diptych's
facing panel—wide-eyed acolyte,
urgent petitioner

hands clasped over your gilt-
edge book. Which once saved me.
Now my devotions

must be sure, pure enough
that I will be able to see
myself transported to

your panel, deep
in its background where
we appear to share

one space in the convex mirror.
Let it be so.
This late renaissance.

SÉANCE

Only connect . . .

Between conditions suitable & . . . . *not suitab*
   locate the difficulty . . . .   the shining garment
                                   tightrope of fire that crosses
                                palm—to—palm

Smell an art or alluring swindle
Nothing up the dream sleeve?

                             palm . . . . lamp

Between illusion & essence . . .
  The unexpected, while capable of occurring,
may be unaccepted.
              You tell me where
                the rest of her . . . . body has   gone

           joinhandsjoinhandsjoinhands!

Between silence & speaking . . . . a forlorn horn
                        moan of the spellbound
                          harp in a corner plucked by

Stray thought—present conditions dingy—
     caught
    for a moment before
     wriggling free
        look . . . .   something oozes from her earrrrrrrrr
                             her parting part
                                 ecto- see?

Between stars & sea
the plank where Reason walked
before breaking   to make   this table th tha that   rises a raft on air

(what is it?)   materialized slipper on the medium's head
            grief—coin—palm—bread
It taints so.

76

Curtains split for a spectral hand

Say anything now . . . .

dead father   dearest aunt

Let go.   Let go.   Let go . . .   .

Oh don't

Rite of Ten

Splash fingers in brackish water often
Let bleakness descend upon your shoulders often
Make dimes leak right from your pocket often
Disable engines of coercion often
Arrange daisies in an epergne often

Let love disregard conclusion often
Turn pages of a blank book often
Wait for yeast to increase dough often
Lubricate the small gears of minutes often
Remember often your dues to those left dead.

UNDERWORLDLING

What'd he say? What'd anybody
Say—I'm not paid to parse cacophony.

Enough that their soles pound over my head
Like the rudest neighbors you ever had.

A scream in time, a screw to fit the thumb,
I'm down with the dug, I'm depth to plumb.

The dearth of me, with dirt in hand, all grunge,
A bump in nadir's lightless bungee plunge.

I serve, yes, majesty—what trifle I earn
I deserve. No booty left round here to burn.

Congested I bed twixt roots and the dead.
My digs are too dense for dancin', instead

I sing my song to crack ears, curdle tongues,
Summoning those who least want to come home.

YOU ARE ASH

You hay our horse
You oar our shore
You hoe our area
You shear our hero

You hose our soy
You sear our ore
You rosy our rays
You ear our hares

You sour our rye
You hoarse our hearsay
You rue our era
You sue our arse

You shy our rose
You house our eros
You use our hours
You yore our years

You hear our rush
You say our ruse
You rouse our rash
You share our shoe

You has our sore
You hoary our hue
You sure are easy
You so are ash

Rite (to appear as sky and grass)

Open wide
thy cornflower eye   thy violet
embellish danger with moss
wind thy hair throughout a tree
ask emptiness   ask straw

only the grass reads all the sky words

these too like the look of things
wait patiently to be transformed
empty nest   last seed ever sown
to stand without a stand

only sky can read the message pressed in grass

be extravagant   discard thy legs
ask emptiness   ask straw
part the fringe   make way
for the great   & minor wings

thy hush will come in handy now

HOME IN THE WORLD

Sometimes when I'm in countries alone
    I look at the stars.
        Once, in San Gimignano,

where I had placed my feet
    on the footmarks to pee, there
        hung

a huge ecstatic red-orange moon,
    the kind a god would sink
        his shiny teeth into.

It's sky always and everywhere,
    and gravity, too
        that holds me to the skin

of the planet, but not so stringently
    that I cannot lift my feet
        to wander

a little along a path Etruscan soles
    might have trod.
        Entering a domed tomb room

with my meager travel flashlight
    I found niches, bunks in the walls
        for their bodies, which seemed

sensible and cozy, and I climbed
    back out and there—sky,
        and the sun winked loudly,

my eyes juiced like grapes
and I'd burst my skin, also
delicious, also food

for a god as the earth will one day
consume me entire
and refashion my atoms into

a leafy garment for itself. Which is okay.
Our lives must be shaded, must be tilled.
These heavenly bodies never leave me.

RITE (of passage for one set to shepherd millions to greener grass)

your task is to ignite water
your task is to mortify skin

      on a bad day your genius is dormant
      on a bad day you crawl and crow

say your lineage is ascending
your lineage is a clothesline reeling in

      keep a swiss knife in your arsenal
      brandish a corkscrew and thin file

your name is a mispronounced tourniquet
your name is an abused acrostic

      if the shoe falls, make cobbler
      if the skin is flayed, call it kin

in your sorrow-nutshell you wait knotted
in your sorrow forty fetal days

      your body is a propeller of hours
      your body will release its prisoners

your terror's no longer contagious
your terror's no longer mailed in an envelope

      on a good day you have radar for lies
      on a good day your swelling larder

say you made your bridge with discarded crutches
say you made your tunnel with the dreams of voles

you are the gold occasion
you are the fat calf of nation

here is the cave the bloom broke in
here is the capable mouth shouting *rise*

Circumference

Here is an old woman
whose apron pockets sag
with the obduracy of rocks. No,
she is not about to jump
into the river, she is not hunting
wolves or saints.
She is casting a circle on a dry patch of earth,
her face taut as though pulled
with a drawstring,
her hair blue-white like a
fluorescent bulb. She warms
the stones with both hands
mumbling a few minutes
then
lets them fall into place.
The radius of the evolving circle
is the length of an incarnated god.
Each rock displaces
a small exclamation of dust
that's blown right off.
If you sneeze, she won't
bless you. She cannot
hear you at this time.
What you guess you hear—
turbulence turbulence—
is not what she means to say.
After you turn away
you grow afraid to look
back and find she's disappeared.
Look.
An old woman is here.
You have vanished.

NOTES

"An Instantaneous Production" and "The Hooked Gimmick" are names of magic tricks; the poems borrow and corrupt text from *Silken Sorcery* by Jean Hugard.

"Flower & Camera," "Broken Dolls Day," and "Burning of the Three Fires" are all poems marking holidays as found on Web-Holidays.com. Thanks to Elaine Equi for the holiday-poem prompt. Her edited anthology *The Holiday Album* can be found on-line at jacketmagazine.com/32/holiday-album.shtml.

"*[EXIT CORPSE]*" is a collage of sentences and phrases from *The Bell Jar* by Sylvia Plath.

"Channeling Sylvia: 8-Ball (Interrogation)" is a transcript, without editing or re-arrangement, of an actual question & answer session conducted through a Magic 8-Ball with "Sylvia Plath."

Other debts: *La Belle et la Bête* (Cocteau), *Psycho* (Hitchcock), "Home Sewn: Three Centuries of Stitching History" (The New-York Historical Society), The Brothers Grimm, Washington Irving, Hans Memling, *Art Doll Quarterly*, E. M. Forster, "The Perfect Medium: Photography and the Occult" (Metropolitan Museum of Art).

ACKNOWLEDGMENTS

Thank you to the editors who previously published these poems, sometimes in earlier versions:

Barrow Street: "A Vienna Postcard," "Gal Lore," "New Wives' Tales: Index of First Lines," "What She Carry," "Burning of the Three Fires," "Four Seasons," "Séance";
Colorado Review: "Recollections: Aviary," "As If Nothing Happened";
Columbia Poetry Review: "From the Annals of Perseverance," "_____less";
Conduit: "[EXIT CORPSE]";
Court Green: "Oranges," "Channeling Sylvia: 8-Ball (Interrogation)," "[EXIT CORPSE]";
Crab Orchard Review: "Broken Dolls Day";
Denver Quarterly: "A Childhood, B.C." "An Instantaneous Production," "Rite (for quitting the premises)";
88: "Your Sign Is Digger";
Ekleksographia: "Rite (to combat a bad mood)," "Rite (of passage for one set to shepherd millions to greener grass)";
Ellipsis: "Reading a Road Map";
The Fairy Tale Review: "Ma Belle," "Is Rain My Bearskin?";
Jacket: "Flower & Camera";
The Journal: "The Birdbath, or Not My Usual Entrance and Exit," "Going by Taxi";
The Manhattan Review: "A Notion," "The Hooked Gimmick";
nycBigCityLit.com: "YOU ARE ASH";
Poetry Northwest: "When I Am in the Kitchen";
Pool: "In Pursuit of the Original Trinket";
Rattapallax: "Taper, or Mary Tells All She Knows";
RealPoetik: "Fancy That Does Not Do But Is," "Poor Shoddy," "If You Wish To Be Removed from This List";
River Styx: "Bride";
Southern Poetry Review: "Getting to Know You," "Screened-in Porch";
The Same: "Underworldling";
U.S. 1 Worksheets: "Dressing Table, 1963," "Who Was the First in Her Class to Finish Her Apron";
Women's Studies Quarterly: "Girl on a Scale";
World Literature Today: "Circumference."

"Getting to Know You" is reprinted in *Don't Leave Hungry: 50 Years of Southern Poetry Review* (U. Arkansas, 2009). It was also printed as a broadside by Boxcar Press for a reading at the Downtown Writer's Center in Syracuse, NY, 2005. "Going by Taxi" was reprinted in *When She Named Fire: An Anthology of Contemporary Poetry by American Women* (Autumn House Press, 2008). "Screened-in Porch" appears in *Family Matters* (Bottom Dog Press, 2005). "Is Rain My Bearskin?" was selected for *The Year's Best Fantasy and Horror 2007: Twentieth Annual Collection* (St. Martin's Press, 2007). "Broken Dolls Day," "Oranges," and "As If Nothing Happened" appeared in the *Poetry Calendar 2008, 2009, 2010*, respectively (Alhambra Publishing). "Removed: A Meditation" appeared in a limited-edition festschrift chapbook *The Gift of Light: Tributes to Donald Sheehan*. "Home in the World" appears in *Letters to the World* (Red Hen Press, 2008). I am grateful to Sharon Dolin, Karen Garthe, Susan Thomas, and Baron Wormser for responding to versions of this book with candor and encouragement.

ABOUT THE AUTHOR

Jeanne Marie Beaumont is the author of two previous poetry collections, *Curious Conduct* (BOA Editions, 2004) and *Placebo Effects*, which was a National Poetry Series Winner (Norton, 1997). Her work has appeared widely in anthologies and magazines including *Good Poems for Hard Times*, *The Year's Best Fantasy and Horror*, *Poetry Daily*, *Boston Review*, *The Nation*, and *World Literature Today*. Her poem "Afraid So" was made into an award-winning short film by Jay Rosenblatt, which has played at numerous international film and literary festivals. With Claudia Carlson, she edited *The Poets' Grimm: 20th Century Poems from Grimm Fairy Tales*. She teaches in the Stonecoast low-residency MFA program and at the Unterberg Poetry Center of the 92nd Street Y, and is director of the annual Frost Place Advanced Seminar. She lives in Manhattan with her husband, two cats and several tribes of dolls.

Website: www.jeannemariebeaumont.com

BOA Editions, Ltd.
American Poets Continuum Series

Colophon

Burning of the Three Fires, poems by Jeanne Marie Beaumont, is set in Adobe Garamond Pro, a digital font designed in 1989 by Robert Slimbach (1956–) based on the French Renaissance roman types of Claude Garamond (ca. 1480–1561) and the italics of Robert Granjon (1513–1589).

The publication of this book is made possible, in part, by the special support of the following individuals:

Anonymous (3)
M. Jan Bender in memory of Pem Bender
Nelson Blish & Sharon Stiller
Gwen & Gary Conners
Mark & Karen Conners
Wyn Cooper & Shawna Parker
Charles & Barbara Coté in memory of Charlie Coté Jr.
Robert L. Giron
Kip & Debby Hale
Janice N. Harrington & Robert Dale Parker
G. Jean Howard
Bob & Willy Hursh
Robin, Hollon & Casey Hursh in memory of Peter Hursh
X. J. & Dorothy M. Kennedy
John & Barbara Lovenheim
Fred Marchant in memory of Andrew Grene
Elissa & Ernie Orlando
Boo Poulin
Deborah Ronnen & Sherman Levey
Steven O. Russell & Phyllis Rifkin-Russell
Vicki & Richard Schwartz
Pat & Mike Wilder
Glenn & Helen William